Signals for survival

JILL BAILEY

HODDER AND STOUGHTON

LONDON SYDNEY AUCKLAND TORONTO

British Library Cataloguing in Publication Data
Bailey, Jill
  Signals for survival.
  1. Animals. Control systems
  I. Title   II. Series
574.1'882

ISBN 0-340-42905-4

Text and illustration copyright © BLA Publishing Limited 1989

First published 1989

All rights reserved. No part of this publication may be reproduced or transmitted in any form or by any means, electronically, mechanically, including photocopying, recording, or any information storage and retrieval system, without either the prior permission in writing from the publisher or a licence permitting restricted copying. In the United Kingdom such licences are issued by the Copyright Licensing Agency, 33-34 Alfred Place, London WC1E 7DP.

Published by Hodder & Stoughton Children's Books,
a division of Hodder & Stoughton Ltd
Mill Road, Dunton Green, Sevenoaks, Kent. TN13 2YJ

This book was designed and produced by BLA Publishing Limited, East Grinstead, Sussex, England.

A member of the **Ling Kee Group**
LONDON·HONG KONG·TAIPEI·SINGAPORE·NEW YORK

Phototypeset in Britain by BLA Publishing/Composing Operations
Printed and bound in Spain

Note to the reader
On page 59 of this book you will find the glossary. This gives brief explanations of words which may be new to you.

Contents

Seasons, signs and signals	6
Rhythms of life	8
Time to sleep	10
Living clocks	12
Daily rhythms	14
Creatures of the night	16
An up-and-down life	18
Signals of the seasons	20
Reading the signals	22
Preparing for winter	24
The long sleep	26
The great shutdown	28
Born survivors	30
Migration — the great escape	32
Why migrate?	34
The mysteries of migration	36
Steering by the sun	38
The dancing bees	40
Making maps	42
Magnetism — the invisible guide	44
Moonstruck	46
Multiplication time	48
Safety in numbers	50
Changing colour	52
Changing shape and style	54
We use signals, too	56
Bibliography	58
Glossary	59
Index	60

Seasons, signs and signals

The world is a very orderly place. Day follows night, spring follows winter, summer follows spring, and autumn follows summer. The moon appears to grow from new moon to full moon, then shrink until it is invisible again every 29.5 days. On the seashore, the tide rises and retreats again every 12.4 hours.

▲ Tree swallows get ready for their autumn migration.

Obeying the rules

Living things have to fit in with this order. If hawks sleep by day and come out to hunt at night, they will not be able to see to find their prey.

In northern countries, the swallows arrive each spring, bring up their families, and fly south every autumn. If they do not fly south at this time, there will soon be no insects for them to eat and they will starve to death.

Apple trees burst into blossom in the spring. If the flowers open in the winter instead, the frost will kill them. Sandhoppers must bury themselves in the sand before the tide comes in, or they will be washed away.

The food hoarders

Many small animals start to hoard food and eat more to prepare for their long winter sleep months before winter arrives. By the time the dormouse starts its winter sleep, 40% of its body weight will be fat. Hamsters stock up their larders with seeds, nuts and mushrooms. A single hamster may store 90 kg (200lb) of food in its burrow.

Gerbils often build large stacks of food outside their burrows. The largest one found measured 3 metres (10 feet) long and was one metre (3 feet) high. How do these animals know when to start hoarding food and fattening up?

◀ A marmot collects dry grass to line his winter nest.

SEASONS, SIGNS AND SIGNALS

Advance warnings

How do plants and animals know when to do what? It is no use a tree producing blossoms on a freak warm day in December, when frost will form at night. If the sandhopper waits until it feels the splash of the incoming tide, it will be swept away before it can burrow into the sand. So there must be signals which give advance warning of the changes that are coming.

Some of these signals are obvious. You can tell the time of day, even without a watch, by the brightness of the sunlight. Even on a cloudy day, it gets brighter from dawn until midday, then darker as the afternoon goes on. In countries some way north and south of the equator, you can tell the time of year by the lengths of day and night. Days are longer and nights shorter in summer.

▲ Apple trees and buttercups bloom in the spring.
▼ The badger's internal clock tells it when to wake up.

But sunlight cannot warn us about all the changes in our surroundings. For instance, how do you know the tide is coming in if you are too small to see it? How does an animal living in an underground burrow know it is time to get up? How do the swallows in their winter home in the tropics know that spring is about to arrive further north?

This book will show you some of the many signals used by plants and animals to help them survive in this ever-changing world. It will explain why the signals are important, and how living things respond to them.

More about ▶ Advance warnings p 20-23, 29, 36-37 Seasonal rhythms p 15, 22-25, 32-37, 48-49
Moon and tide p 8-9, 46-47 Internal clocks p 12-14, 16-19, 28, 30, 49, 56-57

Rhythms of life

If you are reading this book, then you must be awake. And if you are awake, there is a good chance that it is either daytime or early evening, because most people sleep at night. They find it difficult to sleep in the middle of the day, and difficult to stay awake all night.

A time for action

Most animals have definite patterns of sleeping and waking. At certain times of day they are active — feeding, mating, defending their territories, or looking after young. At other times they are asleep, or at least inactive, hiding in a sheltered place.

Most birds feed by day, using their eyes to find their food. The fading light of evening makes them return to their roosting places to sleep. Birds have been 'tricked' into flying home to roost in the middle of the day during an eclipse of the sun.

In the oceans, many small creatures like spider crabs and feather stars, come out to feed at night. In the daytime, they would soon be spotted by hungry fish.

Space for everyone

Because some animals come out to feed at night and others feed by day, more animals can live together in the same place. Birds like flycatchers, warblers, tits and chickadees feed on insects by day, and insect-eating bats feed on them by night. The large fruit-eating bats of the tropics often roost out in the open, sometimes sharing a tree with the birds. The birds occupy the tree at night, and the bats roost there in the daytime.

Day-active (diurnal) and night-active (nocturnal) animals use different ways of finding food. Animals that feed at dawn and dusk, or at night, have large eyes for seeing in dim light, or use other senses to find their food. Badgers and hedgehogs sniff the ground for smells of food. Bats hunt moths by uttering high-pitched cries and listening for the sound to bounce back from the moth's body. Diurnal animals usually have sharp eyesight, and some have colour vision, too. Because they can see clearly where they are going, some animals, like cheetahs and hares, can move very swiftly. Animals are specialized for different activity patterns, adding to the variety of life.

◀ Fruit bats roost by day in a tree in Nepal. The same tree may be used by roosting birds at night.

RHYTHMS OF LIFE

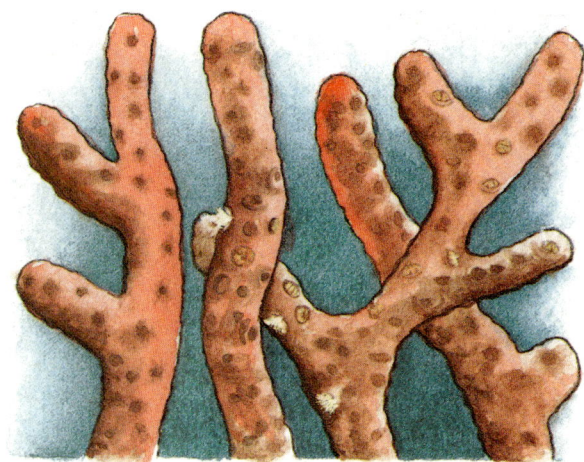

Rocks by day, animals by night
Corals come out to feed at night. Their soft bodies emerge through tiny holes in their rocky skeleton, looking like miniature sea anemones with rings of stinging tentacles. If you shine a torch on them, they pull in their tentacles and retreat out of sight.

Sharing out the food
Seasonal rhythms are also important. In the far north, millions of insects breed in the pools formed by the melting snow in spring. Many birds, such as warblers and swallows, spend the winter in the tropics and sub-tropics. They migrate north for the summer, to take advantage of the plentiful food and longer summer days to rear their families. This gives the resident tropical birds — thrushes, finches, flycatchers, tanagers and many others — a chance to rear their young while there is less competition for food.

◀ Bushbabies have the large eyes typical of a nocturnal mammal.

More about — Sleep p 10-12, 17, 26-28, 56 Diurnal and nocturnal animals p 16-17, 30 Migration p 32-37, 42-43, 54

Time to sleep

When animals are not actively searching for food or mates, they are often asleep. Most animals, including humans, sleep for about the same amount of time every day, at the same time of day. A natural 'clock' inside the body tells it when to sleep and when to awaken. It is hard to ignore this clock, as you find out if you try to stay up late at a party, or if you have to get up in the night to go to work, like nurses and other shift-workers.

▲ Small mammals lose heat easily once they stop moving around. They sleep curled up in a ball, with the thick fur on their backs on the outside. Squirrels wrap their bushy tails around them like fur coats.

▼ The parrotfish spends the night asleep in a mucus cocoon, which may help to hide it from its enemies.

What is sleep?

When we are asleep, we are not aware of what is going on around us. Our eyes are closed, and we do not hear nearby noises. But sleep is not simply being unconscious. In fact, a sleeping animal will usually react to sounds or smells of danger by waking up. During sleep, the muscles relax, and the temperature of the body falls. The animal's heart beat slows down, and its breathing becomes slower and deeper. That is why you can often hear a sleeping animal breathing. The animal becomes less aware of hunger and thirst, and its urine flow slows down, so that its sleep is not interrupted.

TIME TO SLEEP

Do all animals sleep?

It is difficult to tell if animals like slugs and snails sleep. Certainly most vertebrates (animals with backbones) sleep. Pet dogs usually curl up in their baskets when the rest of the family goes to bed. Cats, however, will doze in front of the fire even during the daytime.

Giraffes find it difficult to lie down and get up, so they often sleep standing up. Birds tuck their heads under their wings to sleep, and bats hang upside down. Swifts are said to sleep on the wing, soaring through the air 2000 metres (6000 feet) above the ground. Fish have no eyelids, so they sleep with their eyes open. They often rest quite still at the bottom of the pond or sea bed.

Why do we sleep?

No-one really knows why we need to sleep. Some think it gives the brain time to sort out its thoughts by dreaming. In animals, sleep provides a way of keeping an animal out of trouble at a time when it cannot usefully move around. For example, an animal that relies on sight to find its food will sleep at night, when it cannot see. By sleeping, it keeps still and quiet, so it does not attract the attention of predators. Each animal has its own special time for waking and sleeping, suited to its way of life.

Sleeping at sea

Manatees (sea cows), whales and seals can sleep under the water, occasionally coming to the surface to breathe without even waking up. Sea-otters and sea-lions sleep floating in the water, keeping their noses in the air to breathe. The sea-otter will wind seaweed around itself like a blanket in order to prevent it from drifting too far away from the shore.

▼ Young animals often sleep for much longer periods than their parents. Human babies are no exception.

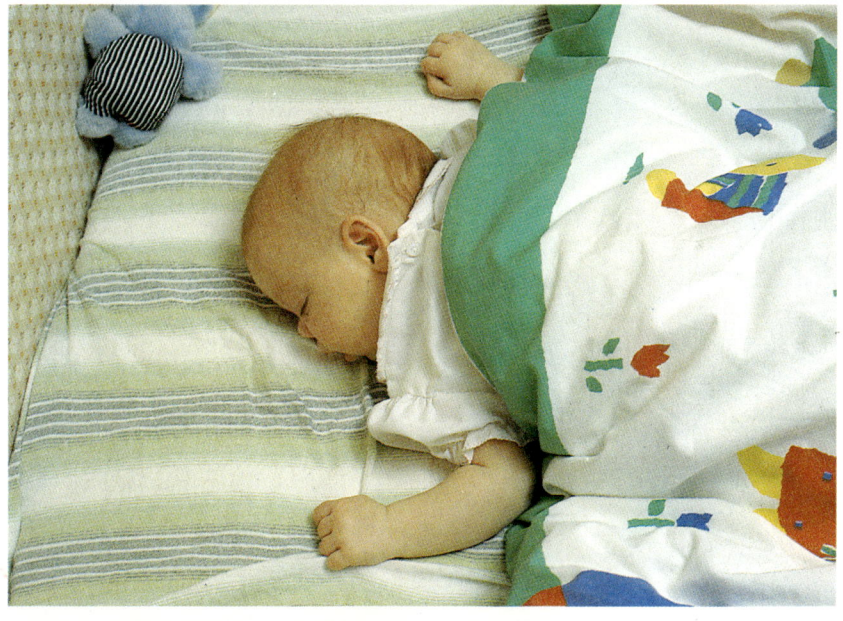

More about ▶ Sleeping fish p 31 Sleep p 12-13, 17, 24, 26-28, 31, 56
Sleep records 17, 27 Daily rhythms p 12-15, 18-19, 53, 56-57

Living clocks

▲ At night, the sensitive plant folds its delicate leaves.

Animals have daily rhythms of waking and sleeping, and annual (yearly) rhythms of breeding. Plants may have daily rhythms of opening and closing their flowers, and annual ones of flowering and fruiting. Even microscopic organisms have daily rhythms of chemical processes in their cells. All living things show rhythms in their life processes.

Time signals

What makes an animal active at a particular time of day and inactive at another time? Does it sense the change in light intensity at dawn and dusk and respond to them? Humans often find it difficult to go to sleep if the sun is shining or the room is not darkened, but it is easy to doze off even in the daytime in a darkened room.

It is not as simple as that. If humans stay in a dark cave where they cannot see the light, they still show a cycle of waking and sleeping, whether they are active or not. Animals such as foxes and voles, which live under the ground, still wake up at dawn, even though they cannot see the light. It is as if they have some sort of internal clock.

Plants also seem to have internal clocks. The sensitive plant has leaves that fold up at night. Even if the plant is placed in constant light or darkness, and constant temperature, the leaves still open and close at regular times. They seem to know if it is morning or evening.

LIVING CLOCKS

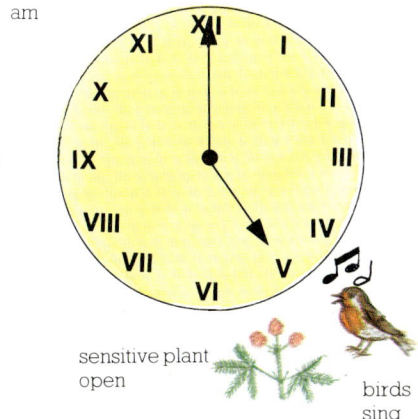

sensitive plant open

birds sing

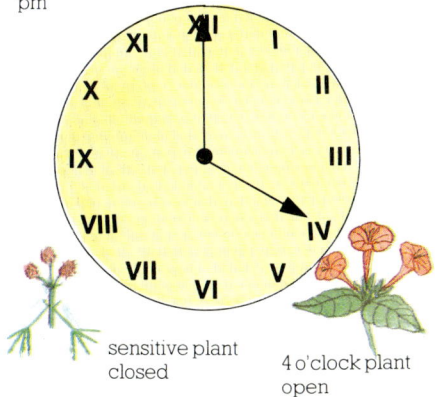

sensitive plant closed

4 o'clock plant open

How a biological clock works

If plants or animals are kept in the dark, their daily rhythms drift away from an exact 24-hour pattern. Some become 25-hour rhythms, others 23-hour rhythms.

Humans kept in a dark cave woke up and went to sleep at a slightly later time each day. Their cycle of waking and sleeping became 25 hours instead of 24 hours. On their return above ground, when they could see the daily changes in light, their sleep cycle returned to 24 hours. So it seems that humans have an internal clock which can programme body rhythms to around 24 hours. But this clock needs external signals like changes in light intensity to adjust its timing and to keep it accurate.

Different body processes have different rhythms. They vary in the length of the cycle — some are daily, some yearly (annual), some even follow the times of the tides or the phases of the moon. The body of a complex animal or plant will contain many different biological clocks.

Keeping time

The position of the hands of a clock on the clock face show you what the time is. The hands of the internal biological clock are the visible signs like activity or sleeping, or the opening and closing of flowers. A clock-maker adjusts the clock's mechanism so that it runs at exactly the right speed. In the same way, signals such as light and temperature set the body's internal clock to run at the appropriate speed to give 24 hours in a day, or 365 days in a year.

▲ Humans kept in the dark find that their sleep cycles gradually become 25-hour cycles instead of 24-hour cycles. They sleep and wake at a later time each day.

More about Biological clocks p 14, 16-19, 28, 30, 49, 56-57
Human sleep patterns p 10-11, 56 Plants that tell the time p 14, 15

Daily rhythms

Because the Earth spins on its axis once every 24 hours, different parts of the globe face the sun at different times of day. If you stand in the same place all day, you will gradually spin away from the sun and into darkness — into night. Ever since living things first appeared on the Earth millions of years ago, they have had to adapt to daily changes in light and warmth.

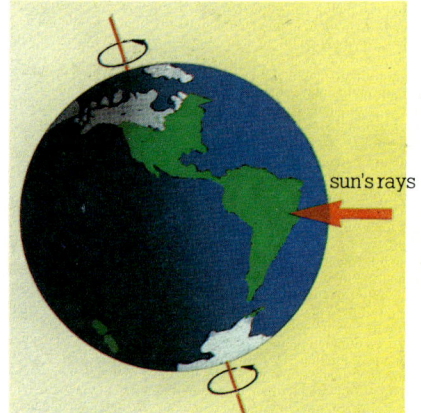

Plants that tell the time

Some plants, like daisies and dandelions, open their flowers by day and close them at night. Flowers attract insects like bees and butterflies to feed on their sweet-smelling nectar. Pollen sticks to the insects' hairy bodies, and rubs off on the other flowers they visit. A flower must receive pollen from another flower in order to produce seeds. Most insects are active only during the day, so the flower would not profit by remaining open

▲ In the daytime, a bee visits flowers to collect pollen. Its hairy body becomes covered in tiny yellow pollen grains.

at night. By closing, it protects the delicate stamens that produce the pollen.

Other flowers, like the evening primrose and the tobacco, read the light signals differently. They open at night and close by day, since they use night-flying moths to carry their pollen.

Early birds

In the early morning, birds use their internal clocks to wake up. Once awake, they use the light signal to start their dawn chorus. The early morning is a good time to sing, because there is usually very little wind then, so the sound carries a long way. In any case, this time of day is not very good for feeding. The light is not bright enough to spot seeds, and insects do not come out until the air has warmed up.

DAILY RHYTHMS

The singing season

There is another rhythm involved in the dawn chorus, a seasonal one. You will not hear much of a dawn chorus from mid-summer to late autumn. Then it will start very gradually, with just a few birds singing, until it swells to a maximum in spring. This is because most birds breed in the spring and summer.

During the winter, special chemicals (hormones) are produced inside the bird to make it ready to breed in spring. Male birds sing mainly to warn other birds off their territory, the patch of land in which they find food and bring up their families. By late summer, when the bird has reared its family, the hormones change again. The bird is no longer in 'breeding condition', and it loses the urge to sing.

▲ Bluetits breed in the spring, when the lengthening days tell them it is time to raise a family.

Weather clocks

Daisies and dandelions will also close when clouds shade the Sun. This helps to protect them from the rain to come. The scarlet pimpernel opens only when it is really sunny, and is often called the poor man's weatherglass. The four o'clock plant flowers exactly at tea-time every day, and probably uses an internal clock.

More about ▸ Seasonal rhythms p 22-25, 32-37, 48-49 Breeding birds p 37, 48-50
Daily rhythms p 12-13, 18-19, 53, 56-57

Creatures of the night

▲ Badgers sniff for food as the evening light fades.

As day passes into night, the light decreases, the temperature falls, and the water in the air condenses into droplets, forming dew. So night time is cooler and moister than daytime. This means that plants and animals can use light, temperature or moisture to tell them whether it is night or day. At night, sounds and smells carry further as there is often less air movement. They can be used to send messages from one animal to another, track prey and warn of danger.

Keeping moist

Small animals like slugs, snails and earthworms can lose water easily through their body surface. They only come out to feed at night, when the air is cool and moist. Predators like shrews and hedgehogs, which feed on slugs, snails and worms, must therefore hunt at night, too. They also benefit from the darkness, which hides them from *their* enemies. Hedgehogs and shrews rely on smell rather than sight to find their prey in the dark.

Telling the time in the dark

In an underground burrow, an animal cannot see when the light fades. Some nocturnal animals may use the falling temperature as a signal to wake up, but many use an internal clock instead. If earthworms are kept in the dark for several days on end, one would expect them to stay out feeding all the time, but they do not. They still return to their burrows when it would normally be daytime, and come out to feed at 'night', proof that they use some sort of biological clock. In the daylight, the worms would risk drying out if they left their burrows, and they would also be easily seen by hungry birds.

▼ Slugs come out to feed when the air is cool and moist.

CREATURES OF THE NIGHT

▲ Lions have few enemies, and can afford to sleep for 14 hours a day.

Safety in numbers
Some nocturnal animals synchronize their internal clocks. If you stand near a bat cave at dusk, you will find that most of the bats leave at the same time. There is safety in numbers — if there is a predator around, like an owl or a bat hawk, it can catch only one bat at a time. If hundreds of bats all leave the cave together, only one will be caught. It pays to get up at the right time!

Sleep records
Humans spend about a third of their lives asleep. The giraffe, which has to keep a constant watch for predators, sleeps for about 20 minutes a night, in snatches of about 5 minutes each. Lions, which have few enemies, can sleep for 14 to 15 hours a day. The opossum may well hold the sleep record — 19 hours a day. The European hedgehog comes a close second, at 18 hours a day. In winter it may sleep for 24 hours a day.

▶ At nightfall, bats all leave their caves at the same time.

More about — Nocturnal animals p 8, 9, 42 Safety in numbers p 50-51 Hedgehogs p 8, 26 Bats p 8, 11, 26

An up-and-down life

Coral climbers

On coral reefs, spider crabs climb on to corals to feed at night. They spread out their bristly legs in the water currents to trap passing food particles. At dawn, when the sun's rays start to filter through the water, the crabs crawl down to deeper water. They sometimes descend over 1 km (0.6 mile). Here, they hide in crevices or under the stinging tentacles of sea anemones, out of reach of hungry fish and squid. If you shine a torch on them at night, within 30 seconds the crabs will stop feeding and start their descent.

◀ Like spider crabs, feather stars climb on to coral pinnacles at night.

▼ A ghost crab heads for its burrow as the incoming tide approaches.

Some animals spend most of their lives going up and down. Earthworms burrow into the soil in the daytime, and travel to the surface to feed at night.

On the beach, burrowing at the right time is even more important. Many small seashore animals, like ghost crabs and sandhoppers, feed on the beach when the tide is out. They must burrow before the tide returns to avoid being swept out to sea. As they need to burrow *before* the tide comes in, the waves are no use as a signal. They have to use an internal clock.

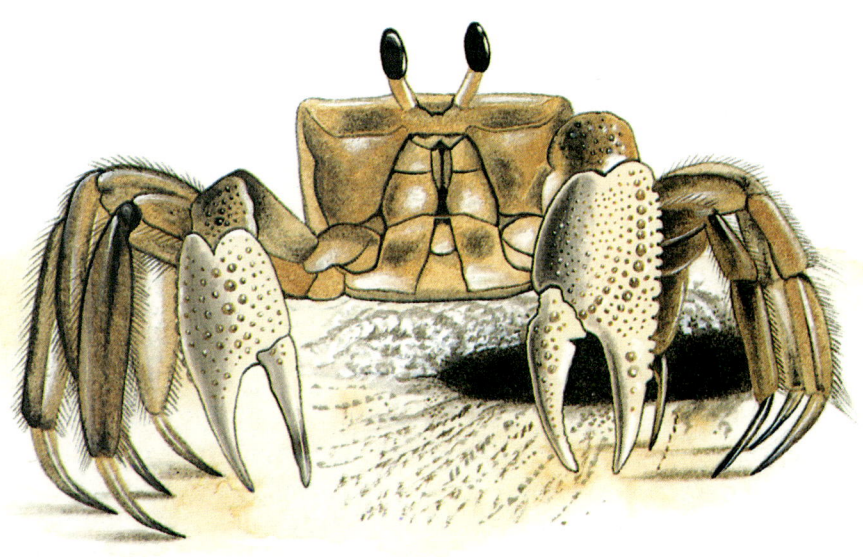

AN UP-AND-DOWN LIFE

▲ This flashlight fish from the East Indies migrates 100 metres (330 feet) into shallow water to feed at night. Special pouches under its eyes produce flashes of light to illuminate its prey.

Sink or swim

Near the surface of the ocean live millions of tiny floating animals, many of them too small to see. They feed on microscopic algae called diatoms, or on each other. This floating community is called plankton.

Many plankton animals move into deeper water in the daytime. Some prawns spend the day 1.7 km (1 mile) down, and swim back to the surface at dusk. By avoiding sunlit waters, they are less likely to be eaten by fish and squid.

For most plankton, the changes in light intensity at dawn and dusk trigger these daily movements. Some use an internal clock to time their travels, adjusting their clocks according to the timing of dawn and dusk. Others simply respond to bright light by swimming away from it. Many plankton animals seem to stay at the same level of light intensity. On overcast days or in cloudy water, they come nearer to the surface than on sunny days or in clear water.

Long-distance commuters

Some deep-water fish also come to the surface at night to feed on the rising plankton. Lanternfish may rise over 1 km (0.6 mile) at night. They spend almost half their lives commuting. Some plankton animals only 1 mm (0.039 in) long travel up and down over 500 metres (1650 feet) a day. This is equivalent to a man travelling nearly 1000 km (620 miles) each way.

Biting time

Mosquitoes also lead an up-and-down life. They like to stay where the air is fairly moist, but not too wet. The air is damp nearer the ground, but at night its moisture increases, so the mosquitoes fly higher to find less moist air. This brings them within reach of exposed human skin. So mosquitoes bite more in the evening and early morning than at midday.

More about — Sinking and swimming p 36, 55 Ups and downs p 33, 39
Signals in the sea p 37, 45, 51, 54 Migration in the sea p 33, 34, 37, 54

Signals of the seasons

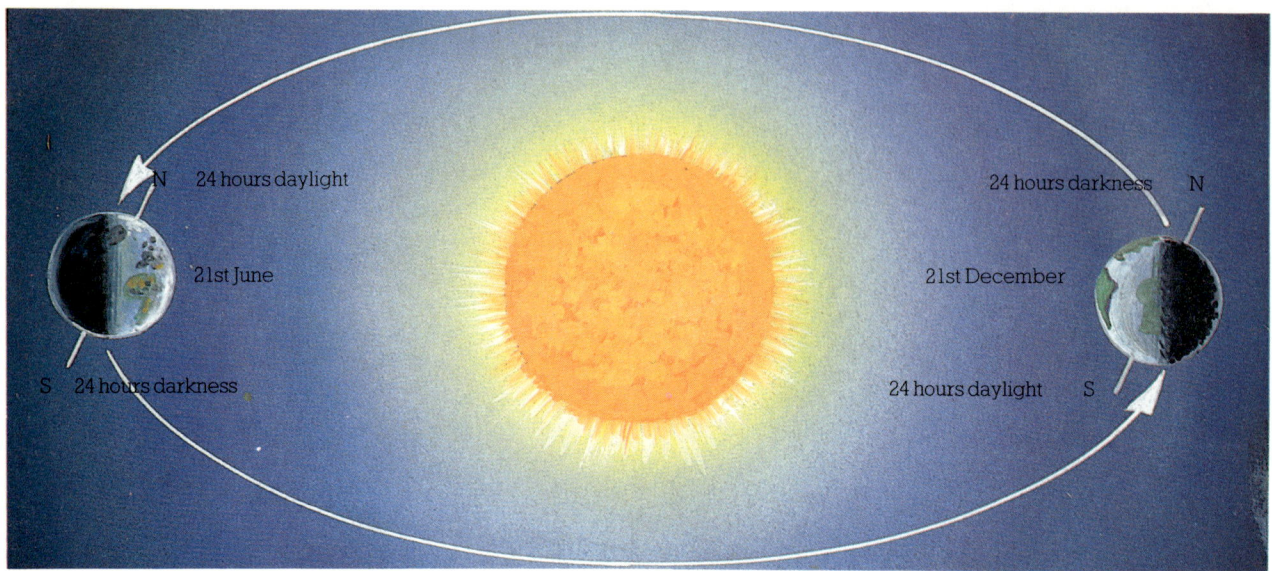

▲ At the poles, day length changes dramatically with the seasons. The equator has almost equal day and night all year.

The Earth takes one year to travel around the sun. As it travels, it spins around its axis, an imaginary line which connects the north and south poles. This spinning causes night and day. At the poles, the sun's rays have to pass through a greater thickness of atmosphere than at the equator, so they are weaker when they reach the Earth's surface. So the poles are cooler than the equator.

Source of the seasons

The Earth's axis is tilted. This means that the north pole is in constant light in summer, and constant darkness in winter. The south pole has winter while the north pole has summer. At the equator, there is equal day and night all year round. Closer to the poles, the days become longer in summer, shorter in winter. Since the sun's rays bring warmth as well as light, this creates the seasons.

▼ In northern countries, the sun is low in the sky in winter and casts long shadows.

The differences in the amount of heat received by the atmosphere in various parts of the globe creates different patterns of winds and weather. The tropics are moist and humid all year round, the subtropics have wet and dry seasons, and temperate regions have warm summers and cool winters.

SIGNALS OF THE SEASONS

◀ The mountain goat's thick winter coat takes many weeks to grow.

Threats to survival

The seasons affect the lives of plants and animals. They bring changes in light intensity, temperature, day length, wind direction and strength, the moisture in the air, fog, rain and snow.

Plants need light in order to grow. They do not grow well if the light is weak or the days are short. Animals that feed on plants may starve, and the animals that feed on them will also starve. Many animals and plants cannot survive the cold of winter, the heat of a desert summer, or the water shortage of a dry season. They need to be warned in advance of these seasons in order to take avoiding action, like storing food, putting on fat to prepare for hibernation or migration, or producing antifreeze chemicals in their bodies.

Warning signals

Temperature is an unreliable signal. In temperate regions, there can be unexpected warm days in winter, and sudden frosts in early summer. Changes like migration, storing food and preparing for hibernation take time and need plenty of *advance* warning. Light intensity is also unreliable, as it changes with the weather. Day length is much more useful. For a given part of the world, the day length is always the same at a particular time of year. The days grow longer in spring, and shorter in autumn.

In desert areas, rainfall is erratic. Desert birds respond to the sight of rain or green vegetation, which signals that there will soon be enough food around to rear a family.

Day length is less important in the oceans. Water heats up and cools down more slowly than land, so seasonal temperature changes are more gradual, and more reliable as signals.

▲ Desert weaver birds start to build their nests when green vegetation appears after rain. This signals that there will soon be enough leaves around to build a nest.

More about ▶ Hibernation p 26-27 Migration p 32-37, 39, 42-43, 49, 54
Desert animals p 30-31, 35, 48

Reading the signals

The commonest seasonal signal used by living things is day length. This may be the actual day length, or the way day length is changing — whether days are getting longer or shorter. Sometimes only one day of the correct length will trigger events such as courtship and mating, migration, or flowering. Sometimes several such days are needed.

The day length acts like a switch. For example, it may switch leaf production to flower production, or normal bird behaviour to courtship or migration behaviour.

Measuring the night

Many flowers of temperate regions bloom in spring or summer. Lengthening days signal that summer is coming. Irises flower in summer, in long days. When the days are long, the nights are short.

▲ The lengthening days of spring bring bluebonnets and coreopsis into flower on a Texas prairie.

Which is most important, day length or night length? If irises are given short days they do not flower. But, if they are given short days, and the long night is broken by a flash of light, they flower. The plant has 'read' a short night. Plants like cocklebur, which flower in the autumn, and primroses which flower in early spring, require long nights which go with shorter days.

The leaves 'read' the light signal. So long as just one leaf receives the right signal, the plant will flower. Some kind of message has passed from the leaves to the buds telling them to produce flowers.

READING THE SIGNALS

Playing safe

Using day or night length as a signal has its drawbacks. Apples and pears will blossom when the days start to lengthen in spring, but may be killed by an early frost. Sometimes more than one signal is used for safety.

Seeds of wheat and barley germinate (sprout) very early in spring, when the ground heats up. But there may be warm spells in autumn. If the seeds germinate then, the young seedlings will be killed by the winter frost. In fact, the seeds will only germinate if they have had a period of cold winter weather first. The chilling produces changes in the seeds which allow them to 'read' the warm temperature signals in spring.

Seeing without eyes

Surprisingly, many insects, mammals and birds do not use their eyes to read day length signals. Instead, the light filtering through the skin and skull is detected directly by a special part of the brain, a sort of clock centre. If house sparrows have caps painted on their heads, they do not breed in spring, even though their eyes are uncovered.

Humans and some other mammals do use their eyes. But the signals from the eyes pass along a special route to the clock centre, not the route taken by ordinary sight signals.

Avoiding confusion

Many animals use the day length signal. Some birds, such as warblers, swifts and swallows, migrate north when the days lengthen in spring. They do not migrate north in autumn, even though the days are the same length as in spring. This is because they need a period of short days (autumn and winter) before they can respond to long days. The short days act like a safety catch on the migration switch.

◄ Snow geese form huge flocks as they migrate north in spring.

| More about | The day length signal p 20-21, 25, 29, 36-37, 49, 51, 52, 56-57
Seeds p 28-29, 31 The time of breeding p 9, 37, 47-51, 57 |

Preparing for winter

▲ Bluebells flower in the spring before the woodland trees spread their leaves and shade them.

Winter is a dangerous time for many plants and animals. Frost can kill tender plants and small animals. Food is in short supply and water is often frozen. The days are short, so there is little time to search for food. These problems can be overcome in many ways, but they all take time. So, plants and animals need good warning that winter is approaching.

Winter underground

Frost does not reach far underground. Seeds buried in the soil are safe from the winter cold, and so are the eggs of many insects and other small invertebrates. Some butterflies and moths spend the winter as pupae (chrysalids) buried in the soil or sheltering under the bark of trees, sometimes encased in fleecy cocoons for extra protection. Seeds, eggs and pupae do not grow in winter, so they do not need much food and moisture.

Mammals like badgers, mice, voles and bears spend the winter asleep in their burrows under the ground. Some, such as the ground squirrel, chipmunk and dormouse, enter a very deep sleep called hibernation. By sleeping for most of the winter, they do not need much food.

Escaping winter

Some plants and animals escape winter. Animals like reindeer, birds and butterflies can migrate to warmer parts of the world. Plants have no such choice. They may pass the winter as seeds buried in the soil. Some plants, such as daisies and field poppies, live for less than a year. They produce seeds and die. In spring, new plants grow from these seeds.

Plants like bluebells, daffodils, trilliums and potatoes die back to ground level in autumn. They survive as underground organs — roots, stems, tubers or bulbs all swollen with stored food. In spring, they use this stored food to produce new shoots and flowers.

PREPARING FOR WINTER

Winter coats
Many mammals grow longer, thicker coats of fur for winter, to keep out the cold. This fur growth is triggered by the decreasing day length and falling temperature in late summer. The wolf, the grizzly bear and the polar bear grow fur up to 65 mm (2.5 in) long. Small mammals like mice cannot grow very long fur, or they would trip over! They often shelter in underground burrows instead.

◀ Yaks grow thick winter coats to protect them from the cold Himalayan winds.

Living antifreeze
Some plants and animals, especially insects, produce antifreeze chemicals in their bodies to prevent them from freezing in winter. The falling temperature of late summer switches on the production of antifreeze. Many trees can survive winter temperatures, but if they are given such temperatures in summer, they will die because they have not yet made their antifreeze.

Some Arctic insects can survive temperatures of −50°C (−58°F), and even North American frogs like the spring peeper can survive temperatures of −10°C (14°F). Frozen frogs lie stiff and still, without breathing. They cannot see. They do not move if pinched, and if injured they do not bleed. Yet they are still alive.

▲ Some trees survive temperatures well below freezing by producing their own antifreeze.

More about ▶ Winter coats p 21, 52 Preparing for winter p 6, 21
Escaping from winter p 23, 32-33

25

The long sleep

Animals get their energy from their food. But when food is scarce in winter, they may spend a lot of energy searching for it. Sleeping through the winter saves energy, and helps animals avoid starvation.

The hibernators
Mammals and birds also use energy to keep themselves warm. Their bodies are designed to work at a specific temperature, which is under the control of a 'thermostat' in the brain. In cold weather they use up a lot of energy keeping warm.

Some small mammals, like mice, squirrels, hedgehogs and bats, hibernate in the winter. Their temperatures fall, and their breathing and heart beats slow down. The dormouse's heartbeat slows from 300 beats to 10 beats a minute. The hibernating European hedgehog can go for up to 150 minutes without breathing. A mammal can save up to 80% of the energy it uses when awake and active.

Sleep signals
Hibernators need to start storing fat or food well before winter sets in. Decreasing day length or falling temperatures may switch on this behaviour. Food shortage is also very important. A well-fed animal will not hibernate. European hedgehogs will stay awake all winter if well fed, while African hedgehogs, which do not normally hibernate, will hibernate if starved.

◀ Dormice hibernate, using their tails as a fur wrap. Dormice sleep so deeply that they can be rolled along the ground like a ball without waking up.

Food for sleep
While they hibernate, these animals live on the food stored in layers of body fat. Before they hibernate, they feed a lot, and their body chemistry changes so that they put on fat more easily. By autumn, half the dormouse's weight may be fat. Hibernating mammals may also store food like nuts and seeds in their burrows to eat if they wake up during the winter.

▲ A hamster uses its large cheek pouches to carry seeds home to stock up its larder for winter.

THE LONG SLEEP

▲ A red squirrel takes a mid-winter snack. Hibernating animals wake up from time to time to stretch their legs or nibble some food. They do not usually sleep for more than two or three weeks at a time.

Record sleepers
Sloths, opossums and armadillos hold the sleep records, spending up to 80% of their lives asleep. The hibernation record is held by the Barrow ground squirrel of Alaska, which hibernates for 9 months of the year. The golden-mantled ground squirrel is said to sleep so soundly that it can be tossed and caught like a ball while it is hibernating.

Safe from the cold
During hibernation, the body temperature falls drastically. This saves energy. In some bats, the body temperature can fall below 0°C (32°F). Bats hibernate in caves, where temperatures do not drop too much in winter.

Other mammals make warm winter nests of grass and leaves. Mice, squirrels and chipmunks curl up in a ball to sleep, exposing only the thick fur on their backs to the cold air. Marmots and gerbils sleep huddled together for warmth.

If they do start to get too cold, hibernating mammals automatically wake up and move around to get warm.

▶ The brown bear gives birth during her long winter sleep, and her young cubs suckle while she dozes. By the time she wakes up in spring, they are big enough to explore the world outside the den.

Or they will warm up by shivering. In order to shiver, the muscles burn up food, and this produces heat.

A cold sleep
Unlike mammals, animals like frogs, salamanders, snakes and turtles cannot produce their own heat. They may also sleep through the winter, but they have to rely on the outside temperature to wake them up. If it gets too cold, they will die.

More about ▶▶ **Heavy sleepers** p 28-29, 31, 35 **Getting fat** p 6, 36 **Snakes** p 30, 35 **Turtles** p 28, 37, 49

The great shutdown

All animals save energy at certain times of the day by sleeping or resting. While they rest, they slow down their body processes to save energy. Some animals and plants can almost totally shut down their life processes to survive difficult times of year — they become 'dormant'.

Heavy sleepers

Small animals lose heat more easily than large ones. Many small birds and mammals enter a kind of heavy sleep, called torpor, if they get too cold. As in hibernation, this saves heat and energy. But this is not true hibernation, because the temperature of their body does not fall far, and their internal clock wakes them up again within a few hours or a few days. Some hummingbirds enter torpor every night, and many small mice and marsupials enter torpor on cold nights.

A shortage of food can also bring on torpor in animals. The whippoorwill, which migrates to North America in spring, will enter torpor soon after arrival if it suffers a period of bad weather when there are not enough insects around for it to eat.

Sleeping without air
Some turtles actually sleep through the winter in the mud at the bottom of ponds, safe from the ice that forms at the surface. Their body processes slow down so much that they can survive the whole winter without breathing air.

▲ A whippoorwill asleep on a cold night in Nebraska, USA.

The living dead

There are many tales of ancient seeds that sprout and grow. Seeds of Arctic lupin, probably 15 000 years old, were found in the frozen mud in Canada in 1954. When thawed out and watered, they successfully produced shoots and flowers.

Seeds allow many plants to survive cold winters or long dry seasons. Seeds have a tough protective coat and carry a small food store from which to produce new shoots, but the key to their survival is the very low rate at which they use energy. They do not grow or move at all, so they do not use their food stores while they rest.

THE GREAT SHUTDOWN

Waiting for the right time

Many seeds need the right signals before they will germinate. Most seeds need warm temperatures and moisture. Some need to be chilled first, to make sure that warmth is due to the arrival of spring, and not to a freak warm day in winter. Lettuce seeds need light in order to germinate. Their seedlings cannot push through the soil very far, so the seed needs to be sure it is near the soil before germinating.

Early warning systems

Seeds are not the only living things to 'switch off'. Many insects like moths, bugs and crickets survive winter or drought as eggs or resting pupae (chrysalids), protected by tough waterproof coats. Whether or not they become dormant depends on signals received earlier in their lives. Some aphids (greenfly) produce dormant winter eggs only if their grandparents received the right day length. These signals make sure the dormant eggs are produced at the right time.

Waking up

For many seeds, insects and other small animals, waking up from a dormant or resting state takes place after a certain time has passed. Often a new signal such as a particular day length or temperature is needed, or they may need moisture in order to resume normal life.

▲ Convergent ladybirds migrate to winter shelters, to hibernate 2800 metres (8500 feet) up in the Sierra Nevada mountains.

More about Sleep p 8, 10-11, 17, 56-57 Aphids p 39, 55
Surviving the cold p 23-27, 35 Underwater sleepers p 10, 11

Born survivors

▲ The Mojave desert in the USA bursts into bloom after rain.

Deserts are some of the most inhospitable places on Earth. By day, the bare earth heats up rapidly, and at night it can be cold enough for frost. Plants and animals quickly lose water to the hot, dry air. Yet life does survive in deserts.

Keeping cool

Many desert animals like kangaroo rats, gerbils, foxes, scorpions and woodlice only come out to feed at night, when the air is cooler and moister. They spend the day in underground burrows, in sheltered crevices or under stones, using their internal clock to tell them when the sun goes down. Temperature affects the clock — the plains garter snake is nocturnal in hot weather, but at cooler times of year it hunts by day.

Closing the door

Desert snails can survive many years of drought by withdrawing into their shells. The snails seal the opening with a sort of lid and stay put.

Sleeping survivors

Dormant organisms are able to survive remarkably harsh conditions which no ordinary animals or plants could live through. The larvae of certain midges in Nigeria live in very shallow rock pools. When the pools dry up, the larvae dry out, losing up to 92% of their water content. In this state, they can survive the very hot temperatures of the baking rock, up to 100°C (212°F). Even after 10 years, if the larvae are put into water, they resume their normal life within hours.

BORN SURVIVORS

Disappearing acts

Rainfall in the desert is often unpredictable. For months, or even years, the desert may appear dry and barren. Yet within a few days of heavy rain, green shoots are pushing up through the bare soil, insects are emerging, and the newly formed pools are full of tadpoles, small fish and shrimps. Where have they come from?

The answer is that they have been dormant — or 'sleeping'. The shrimps and fish have hatched from eggs dormant in the dried out mud. Water was the signal that woke them up and allowed them to hatch. Desert frogs and toads were sleeping, several metres down in the soil, encased in a cocoon of earth and saliva which prevented them from losing water. Within a few hours, they were crawling to the surface to mate and spawn — hence the tadpoles.

Avoiding false alarms

Seeds of desert plants only germinate if they have enough water. Some have poisons in their coats which must be washed out before they can germinate. Only really heavy rain can wash out enough poison. Other seeds need their surfaces scratched to let in oxygen. This only happens during sudden floods after heavy rain, when the seeds are washed away and scrape along the ground.

▼ An African bullfrog digs in to escape the drought.

Fish out of water

Lungfish are found in many of the warmer parts of the world. When the lungfish's pool dries up, it burrows into the mud, and makes a cocoon of mucus to keep it moist.

As well as having gills for breathing underwater, the lungfish has lungs, so it can breathe air through the opening of its burrow. The African lungfish can survive like this for 9 years. When the rains come, it re-emerges.

More about — Night life p 8-9, 16-17, 19, 42-43, 47 Life in deserts p 21, 35, 48 Sleep records p 17, 27

Migration — the great escape

Every spring, hundreds of birds leave their winter homes south of the equator and fly north, often thousands of miles. They will spend the summer in northern latitudes, perhaps even in the Arctic tundra. Here, they will mate and bring up their young before returning south in the autumn. Such journeys are called migrations.

▶ The greatest long-distance traveller of them all — the Arctic tern lives in perpetual summer.

Following the sun

Some birds cover great distances on migration, often flying 3000 metres (10 000 feet) or more above the ground, out of sight of human eyes. The Arctic tern makes a 65 000 km (40 000 miles) round trip from the Arctic to the Antarctic, migrating from one summer to another, so that it never experiences winter. For more than half the year, it never even sees the sun set.

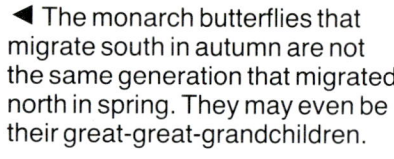

◀ The monarch butterflies that migrate south in autumn are not the same generation that migrated north in spring. They may even be their great-great-grandchildren.

Small travellers

Many insects migrate, too. Butterflies, moths, bugs and aphids will fly north in spring and south in autumn. Or they will fly away from their home area if food becomes scarce. Butterflies are quite strong flyers. Monarch butterflies can keep flying for 117 hours without a stop. Tens of millions of monarch butterflies migrate from northern North America to spend the winter in the southern United States or Mexico. They return north again in spring, a journey of up to 4800 km (2980 miles) each way.

MIGRATION — THE GREAT ESCAPE

Ups and downs of migration

In the mountains of the world, wild goats and sheep, moose, elk and deer move to the shelter of the wooded valleys in winter, and return to graze on the new growth of grass in the mountains in spring. The North American mountain quail spend the summer about 2500 metres (8250 feet) above sea level. When the winter weather comes, they head for the valleys. They are not very good flyers, so they walk down the mountain in single file. In spring they walk up the mountain again.

▲ Coming down the mountain — mountain quail march in single file.

Trails across the continents

Before North America was overrun by settlers, columns of bison 160 km (100 miles) wide migrated from Mexico to Canada, their hooves wearing grooves in the rocks. Today, vast herds of caribou, up to 100 000 strong, march up to 300 km (186 miles) north in spring, crossing rivers and mountains to reach their breeding grounds, courting and mating on the way.

▼ Migrating caribou cross the Kongakut River in Alaska.

In Scandinavia and the USSR their relatives, reindeer, make a similar journey. They spend summer feeding in the Arctic tundra or on high mountain pastures, away from the biting insects of their winter forest home.

Across the oceans

Some of the longest migrations take place across the oceans. The California grey whale migrates about 12 000 km (7440 miles) from its breeding grounds in subtropical Baja to its winter feeding grounds in Arctic waters. The fast-swimming bonito fish travels from the Caspian Sea to southern Africa, and the northern fur seal swims 3000 km (1860 miles) from the Bering sea to the Gulf of Alaska every winter.

 Migration p 9, 21-23, 34-36, 38, 39, 42-45, 49, 54
Butterflies p 24, 38, 53 Following the sun p 39, 41, 43, 45, 54

Why migrate?

Migration uses a lot of energy, and exposes the animals to great danger from exhaustion and bad weather. So why do animals migrate?

Sunseekers

In their summer homes, birds and mammals produce their families. They need plenty of time to hunt for food, and plenty of food to feed their growing young.

Further north, the summer days are longer, giving more time for feeding. After the snow melts in spring, millions of insects breed in the shallow pools of meltwater, food for swallows, warblers and waders. The tender new shoots of grasses, herbs and lichens feed huge numbers of geese, ducks and caribou. There are few resident animals here to compete, as they, too, cannot survive the harsh winter with its frozen ground and lack of food.

▲ The humpbacked whale spends the winter feeding in Arctic waters.

Wandering whales

Most whales spend the winter feeding in cold polar waters. These waters support far more life than the tropical and subtropical waters. Here, the whales feed so well that they put on up to 50% extra weight as blubber (fat).

The whales then travel to warmer waters to give birth to their calves. The newborn calves do not have their parents' thick blubber to protect them from the cold. The whales do not feed from the time they leave their winter homes until they return to them in autumn, a fast of sometimes eight months. During this time, they live off their fat.

▲ Wildebeest migrate in search of fresh green vegetation.

WHY MIGRATE?

Escape from the crowd

Sometimes animals will migrate to avoid overcrowding. Signals of touch and smell become too strong, and many animals leave the area. This prevents the population from eating itself out of food, and gives the animals a chance to colonize new feeding areas.

'Emigrations' like these are common in both rats and lemmings, small vole-like animals that live in Canada and Scandinavia. Hundreds of them leave the area. If the migrating lemmings become crowded in narrow valleys, they seem to panic. Losing their usual caution, they drown in rivers and fall over cliffs as they rush blindly along.

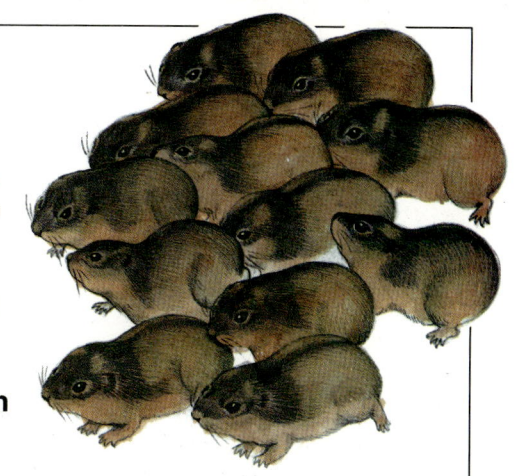

▲ Overcrowding will force young locust hoppers to leave in armies to search for food.

Desert armies

Locust swarms are due to crowding. Locusts are really big grasshoppers. Normally they live solitary lives, quietly feeding on the desert plants. When there has been rain in the desert, and there is plenty of green vegetation, large numbers of locust eggs hatch. The young hoppers become crowded. They respond by forming themselves into armies and marching away, devouring every plant in their path. Eventually they grow into winged adults, and take to the air in vast swarms.

A single locust swarm may contain up to 50 thousand million locusts, and can cover 1000 sq km (386 sq miles), reaching 4 km (2.5 miles) into the sky. A swarm can eat 80 000 tonnes (80 000 tons) of food a day, enough to feed 400 000 people for a year. Locusts use the winds to carry them up to 4500 km (2800 miles) in search of green vegetation.

Stay and sleep

Not all animals migrate. Most cannot fly, and small creatures like mice and beetles cannot run far enough fast enough. Instead, they hibernate in winter or sleep through the dry season. They use special shelters to protect them from the cold, or the sun, and from the eyes of their enemies. Some migrate to and from distant shelters.

In northern latitudes, snakes like adders and garter snakes may travel up to 5 km (3 miles) to communal underground dens. Here they huddle together for warmth and sleep through the winter.

More about — Swallows p 6, 7, 9, 23, 36 Locusts p 48
Whales p 11, 33, 45 Ocean Migrations p 37, 49, 33

The mysteries of migration

▲ Arctic terns cross the oceans to gather at special breeding sites, where there are few predators.

There are many unsolved migration mysteries. Why do some birds migrate and other close relatives stay at home? How do they know where and when to go?

Time to go

Most migrating animals use the lengthening days of spring as the signal to start preparing for their spring migration. First, they need to fatten up. Some birds get bigger appetites than usual, others simply put on fat more easily than usual. Birds may gain up to 40% extra weight before migration. The birds may stop to feed on the way. Swifts and swallows catch insects as they fly. Larger birds seldom need to feed during migration.

Getting lift-off

Many sea creatures make the most of currents and tides for transport. When the current is moving in the wrong direction, they stay on the sea bed. When the current is right, they swim up into the moving water, to be carried where they want to go.

Shrimp larvae make their way into estuaries by swimming when the water is salty, but sinking to the sea bed when it is less salty — where rivers enter the sea. Young plaice will swim when they are hungry, but if they smell food they sink to the bottom to feed.

▼ Migrant warblers only have time to rear one brood a year, but they have large families to compensate.

THE MYSTERIES OF MIGRATION

Insects may respond to changes in temperature rather than day length. Many fish also use the changing water temperature to time their migration. Often they will not migrate if they have not stored enough fat, so the fattest fish leave first.

A built-in timetable

Migrating birds, and probably mammals, too, have a definite sequence of activities through the year, following a kind of internal timetable. This timetable works by changing certain chemical messengers in the body, called hormones. These affect the animal's behaviour, and its responses to various 'signals' it receives from its surroundings.

After the spring migration, the birds court, mate and have their families. Then they lose interest in breeding and start to moult, growing a new set of feathers before the autumn migration. In autumn, many birds do not use the day length signal — migration occurs a certain time after the spring migration, according to the timetable. The birds cannot respond to day length again until mid-winter, when the lengthening days start the whole cycle again.

Maps in the sea

When the ocean currents flow through the Earth's magnetic field, they produce faint electrical currents which can be detected by some fish, a kind of electro-magnetic map. Many sharks and fast-swimming fish like tuna migrate vast distances using an electromagnetic compass. Sharks can detect electrical currents as weak as a flash-light battery connected to two terminals 1600 km (990 miles) apart.

Water currents can also be used for navigating. Some sea turtles travel almost 6000 km (3700 miles) to their breeding beaches. Often major currents follow the same routes as the turtles, and may help them find their way. The migration routes of some turtles are more than 100 million years old.

▶ Leatherback turtles return to the sea after laying their eggs on a beach in Guyana.

More about — Getting lift-off p 39, 55 The timing of migration p 23
Navigating in the sea p 45, 54 Magnetic maps p 41, 44-45, 57

Steering by the sun

▲ A Laysan albatross soars above the Pacific Ocean.

Many animals are remarkably good at finding their way. A Laysan albatross found its way home from Washington State to Midway Island in the Pacific Ocean, a journey of 5150 km (3193 miles), in just 10 days. Migrating monarch butterflies find their winter roosting sites many thousands of kilometres away even though they have never been there before.

◄ Swallows have a remarkable sense of direction. They return to exactly the same nest site every year.

STEERING BY THE SUN

The sun compass

Many animals use the position of the sun as a compass. If ants on their way back to their nest are shown the rays of the sun reflected in a mirror, they change course. When the mirror is removed, they return to their original course.

The sun rises in the east and sets in the west, and it also changes its height in the sky during the day. Animals using a sun compass have to allow for these movements.

Beach sandhoppers use a sun compass to find their way from their burrows to the water's edge. They use an internal clock to allow for the sun's daily movement. At different times of day, they travel at a different angle to the sun. If sandhoppers from Italy are transported to South America, the local time is different, and they run in the wrong direction because they still think they are on Italian time.

Changing course

Many small birds do not live long enough to learn a long migration route. Migrating birds often use a sun compass to navigate by day. The direction they select depends on the time of year — on their annual clock. In spring, they fly north; in autumn, they fly south. Some birds find their winter quarters by flying in a particular direction for a given length of time.

The garden warbler leaves northern Europe in autumn and flies south-west until it reaches the Mediterranean region. It then changes its direction and flies south-east to southern Africa. Young captive birds who have never migrated will hop in a particular direction at migration time. Captive garden warblers hop in a south-west direction for several days, then start hopping south-east. Obviously, they have a built-in flight plan.

Feathered messengers

Homing pigeons have been used for thousands of years. Today they are used mostly for racing, but in the past they were used to carry messages. The ancient armies of Persia, Egypt and Rome used messenger pigeons, and so did the armies fighting in the First and Second World Wars.

Flying at speeds up to 80 km an hour (50 miles an hour), pigeons can travel over 1000 km (620 miles) in a day. They are bred for speed and a good sense of direction — unsuccessful pigeons will tend to end up on the dinner table!

Blue up, yellow down

Some insects use a colour code when migrating. Once an aphid (greenfly) has received the signal to migrate, it becomes attracted to blue — the sky — and takes to the air. After flying for a certain time, it becomes attracted to yellow instead. Green leaves reflect yellow light, so the aphid now flies down to land on a plant. For many insects, the signal to migrate coincides with seasonal winds in a particular direction, blowing them south in autumn and north in spring.

More about | Sun compasses p 40-41 Bird Navigation p 23, 43-45
Sandhoppers p 6, 7, 18, 42, 43, 47 Monarch butterflies p 32

The dancing bees

Honeybees are some of the world's most remarkable navigators. They can even pass on compass directions to other bees. Worker bees have to collect nectar and pollen for all the bees in the hive and for their growing young. So they cannot afford to waste much time looking for suitable flowers.

Making bee-lines

If bees are shut up in their hive for two days, when they are let out they will make straight for flowers that were producing nectar before they were imprisoned. Even after two days, they have remembered the exact place. How do they do it?

Like humans, bees use landmarks like trees or bright patches of flowers to find their way. But how can bees tell each other what landmarks look like? To *remember* the way, they use a sun compass. They note the position of the flower in relation to the position of the sun in the sky and the distance from the hive.

Invisible light

Bees can navigate even when the sun has clouded over, provided they can still see some blue sky. Rays of sunlight are rather like round beams of light. As they pass through the atmosphere, some light rays become flattened in one direction — 'polarized'. By analysing the pattern of polarized light rays, the bees can tell where the sun is. Many animals, such as insects, crustaceans, pigeons, salamanders and goldfish, can see polarized light.

Bee clocks

Some flowers produce nectar only at certain times of day. Bees and butterflies can remember this, and visit these flowers only at the times when they will have nectar. So the bees and butterflies must use an internal clock.

▶ A honeybee flies in search of nectar. Is it using local landmarks, the sun compass, polarized light or perhaps even magnetism to find its way?

THE DANCING BEES

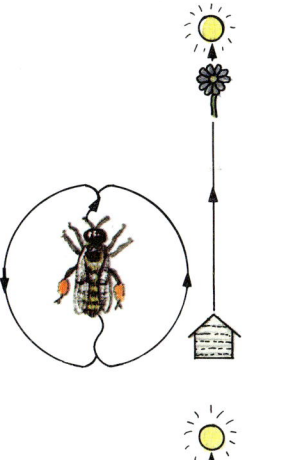

◀ The honeybee waggle dance. The angle made by the straight section of the figure of eight corresponds with the angle the flower makes with the position of the sun.

Telling tales

When a worker bee has found a good source of nectar, she returns to the hive and tells the other workers where to find it. The message is in the form of a dance performed on the vertical surface of the comb. The bee dances in a figure of eight, waggling her abdomen and buzzing as she dances. The position of the figure of eight on the comb is related to the sun compass position of the flower. It tells the other bees what direction to take. The number of buzzes and waggles and the time the dance takes tell the bees how far away the flower is.

The other bees all crowd around the dancer, watching, listening, and touching her with their feelers, probably to smell the scent of the flowers she has visited. Some bees dance for hours on the comb, out of sight of the sky and sun. They gradually change the position of the figure of eight to compensate for the sun's movement round the sky.

Magnetic honeycombs

Honeybee dancers use magnetic information to help them get their dance right. If a magnet is placed near a dancing bee, she will stop dancing. Bees have magnetic material in their abdomens. Wild bees always line up their combs in a north/south direction. They probably 'fix' their north/south direction while they are still pupae in the comb.

◀ A honeybee dancer (centre) performs the waggle dance.

More about — Steering by polarized light p 43 Internal clocks p 12–16, 18–19, 28, 32, 39 Magnetism p 44–45, 57 Insect navigators p 39, 42, 44

Making maps

Birds often migrate at night, or when clouds hide the sun. Some can find their way blindfold. Many fish migrate deep down in the ocean, where the sun's rays are very weak. Ants and other tiny animals can find their way even though they are not tall enough to see very far. These animals cannot be using the sort of maps we have, where hills, valleys and landmarks such as buildings and cliffs mark the way.

The moon compass

Just as some animals use the sun as a compass by day, so many small nocturnal animals use the moon to guide them. Sandhoppers will change direction in response to a torch, and columns of Pharaoh ants marching in line become disorganized if the moon goes behind a cloud.

▲ Canada geese are confused by human direction signs.

▼ Leaf cutter ants lay scent trails to guide them home.

Chemical trails

Some animals, such as leaf-cutter ants, lay a trail of smelly chemicals as they travel away from home. Then they can follow the smell home again. On the seashore, each limpet has its own special patch of rock. Its shell wears a ring-shaped groove in the rock, into which it fits. Limpets leave sticky mucus trails when they go out feeding. They can follow the trail back to their groove even if the home rock is turned round to face another direction.

MAKING MAPS

The star compass

Many animals migrate at night, including many birds that are usually active only in the daytime. They use a star compass. Like the sun, the stars move around the sky during the night, but in a very complex pattern. Birds mainly use a few key constellations — clusters of stars that form an easily recognizable pattern.

In order to test this theory, blackcaps were brought up in constant light so they had never seen a night sky. Then they were put in a planetarium and shown a spring night sky. The blackcaps migrated in a north-easterly direction.

When shown an autumn night sky, they migrated southwest. But they only responded in this way at certain times of year — when their internal clocks told them it was time to migrate.

Learning to find north

The night sky in the northern hemisphere appears to revolve around the Pole Star, which always lies due north of the observer. Another star indicates south in the southern hemisphere. When the birds in the planetarium were shown an artificial sky which revolved around a different star, they still migrated in the right direction — they had learnt the new star compass. Birds probably learn their star compass from the night sky that they see during their first summer.

▲ Limpet shells wear grooves in the rock as their owners settle down after foraging trips.

Master navigator

The sandhopper uses many different compasses. By day, it uses a sun compass, but if the sun goes behind a cloud, it will use polarized light instead. At night the sandhopper uses the moon compass, but if it is cloudy, it works out where the top and bottom of the beach is by the pull of gravity.

More about — Life on the beach p 18, 39, 45-47, 49, 53 Navigating at night p 45 Watching the moon p 46-47, 51, 57

43

Magnetism — the invisible guide

Pigeons can find their way home on cloudy days when they cannot see the position of the sun. Gannets can navigate for hundreds of kilometres over an empty ocean with no landmarks. Thousands of birds migrate on dark cloudy nights when there is no moon, and no stars or landmarks are visible. They must use another kind of compass.

The hidden force

When humans want to find their position on the globe they use a map and compass. This compass is a magnetic one. The compass needle is a small magnet which lines itself up north/south with the magnetic field of the Earth. The Earth is really a very large magnet. It has a north and a south magnetic pole. These poles are not in quite the same position as the geographical north and south poles. The area affected by the Earth's magnetism is called its magnetic field. The magnetic field is particularly strong where there are rocks containing magnetic materials such as iron ore.

▲ Salamanders can find their way home in the dark. Their magnetic compass is several times more accurate than that of the pigeon.

Compass termites

Compass termites live in the dry Australian outback. They build huge mound-like homes, each with two long flat sides and two narrow sides. The short sides always face north and south, so very little surface is exposed to the heat of the midday sun. The larger surfaces face east and west, catching the cooler morning and evening sun. This arrangement helps to keep the mound cool.

◄ Compass termite mounds may be up to 6 metres (19 feet) high, and can house 2 million termites. This is equivalent to a human skyscraper 9 km (29 700 feet) high.

MAGNETISM — THE INVISIBLE GUIDE

Magnetic accidents

Many whales, dolphins and porpoises migrate hundreds of kilometres across the oceans. They follow the pattern of the Earth's magnetic field on the sea bed. Whales are often stranded on certain beaches in considerable numbers. These accident black spots seem to occur where a beach, island or sandbank lies across the path of one of the whale's magnetic 'motorways'.

▲ Misled by magnetism – pilot whales stranded on an Atlantic beach.

Living magnets

Magnetic materials have been found in the living cells of many different organisms — algae, molluscs, termites, honeybees, salamanders, birds, fish, whales, dolphins — and humans.

In birds, magnetic material occurs in the head and in the neck muscles. If a magnet is attached to a pigeon's back, the bird cannot find its way on cloudy days. By placing the magnet in a particular position on the pigeon's head, you can make the pigeon fly in the opposite direction to home. Young birds seem to rely heavily on a magnetic compass. If nestlings are kept in a magnetic field different from that of the Earth, they migrate in the wrong direction in the autumn. Older birds are not so badly affected — it seems that they also have a sun compass.

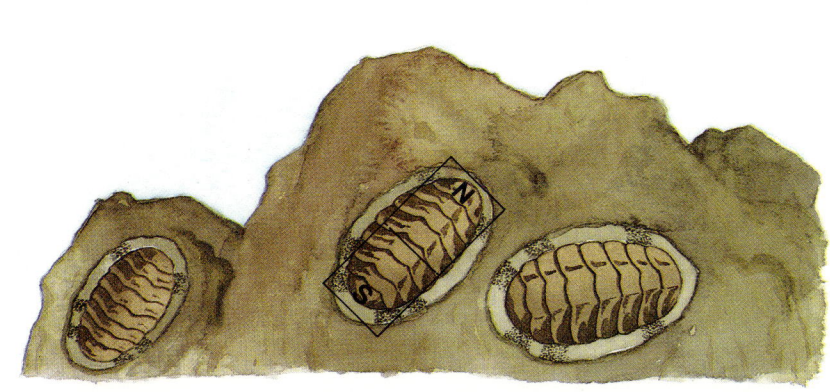

Tongue tracks

Coat-of-mail shells have magnets on their tongues. At night they wander off to feed on algae, but return to exactly the same place on the rock before dawn. Perhaps their tongues help them to find the way. Some coat-of-mail shells always point north when at rest.

More about Whales p 11, 33, 34 Bird migration p 9, 23, 32, 34, 36-39 Navigation p 36-43

Moonstruck

Moon clocks and tide time

Seashore animals can use an internal lunar clock which is synchronized with the phases of the moon to give them warning about the tides. High tides occur twice each lunar day — once every 12.4 hours. The sun's gravity also has an effect. The highest tides, spring tides, form at new and full moon, when both the moon and the sun are in line with the Earth. At quarter moon, the moon and the sun partly cancel each other out, and the tides are at their lowest, neap tides.

Various signals are used to adjust the clock to exactly the right time. Temperature, wave action, and the saltiness of the water all change as the tides surge in and out.

◀ Moonrise over the Chugah Mountains in Alaska.

▼ At new and full moon, the sun, moon and Earth are all in line and the high tides become higher, spring tides. In the moon's first and last quarters, they are at right angles so the tides are smaller, neap tides.

For some animals, especially those that live on the seashore, the moon and the tides play an important part in their lives. The moon circles the Earth every 29.5 days, the lunar (moon) 'month'. The tides are related to the phases of the moon, since they are caused by the pull of the moon's gravity on the water in the oceans.

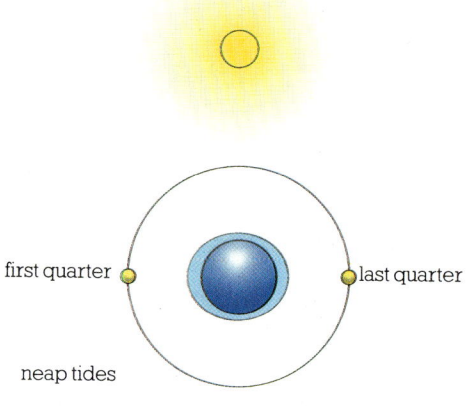

MOONSTRUCK

▲ Hundreds of grunion spawn at the edge of the sea during the highest tides of the month.

By the light of the moon

Horseshoe (king) crabs migrate to the shore to spawn at high tide on low or full moon. These are the highest tides of the month. The eggs are shed into the sand at the water's edge, and develop above the tide level, out of reach of hungry fish. At the next really high tide, two weeks later, they hatch and are ready to drift out to sea.

In California, a small silvery fish called the grunion also spawns at the edge of the sea during the highest tides of the month. The spectacle of beaches being overrun with wriggling fish has become a tourist attraction.

No time to lose

Adult seashore midges live for only 2 hours. They need to lay their eggs on seaweeds which are exposed only at low spring tide, so the midges must emerge about an hour before low spring tide. The signal for emergence of the midges is related to the phase of the moon with the spring tides.

Dangerous moonlight

On land, many nocturnal insects avoid coming out in bright moonlight, in case the light reveals them to their enemies. Some toads also avoid moonlit nights, probably for the same reason.

Staying on the shore

Many intertidal animals use a moon/tide clock. Shore crabs and ghost crabs come out to feed at sunset, whatever the state of the tide. In dim light they cannot be seen by hungry birds. They come out by day only when the tide is in, but run away and hide long before they are uncovered at low tide.

Some shrimps avoid being washed out to sea by the outgoing tide; they burrow in the sand well before low tide. Sandhoppers also use their internal clock to make sure they swim down to the lower beach before the ebbing tide leaves them stranded above high water mark.

More about Tide times p 6, 18, 51 Reproduction in the sea p 34, 49, 51, 55 Fish p 10, 19, 31 Crabs p 18, 53

47

Multiplication time

Have you noticed how the different kinds of animals all seem to produce their young at the same time? Birds usually nest in the spring, lambs appear early in the year, ducklings a little later, and deer fawns later still. The young are born at a time when the weather is not too cold, and there is plenty of food for them.

Attractive repellents

For desert locusts, the signal to start breeding is a highly scented chemical given off by certain desert plants when they burst into leaf after rain. To most insects, this chemical smells unpleasant, and it stops them eating the new leaves. But to locusts, it is an aphrodisiac, and it switches them on to breed!

▲ Red deer fighting during the mating season.

▼ Like deer, sheep mate in the autumn and give birth in the spring.

Getting together

Once a female mammal has mated, and is pregnant, her young will start to grow inside her. For each kind of mammal, the pregnancy lasts an exact length of time. In small mammals, like mice and shrews, the young may be born only 2 or 3 weeks after mating, while large mammals like elephants may have pregnancies lasting nearly 2 years. Obviously, the timing of birth is related to the time of mating. Deer mate in the autumn, which means that they give birth in spring. Birds lay eggs soon after mating, so they do not need to mate until spring comes.

MULTIPLICATION TIME

Switched on and off

Most animals cannot mate all year, or most of the year. Their sexual organs are not fully developed, and need a signal from their surroundings in order to mature.

In birds, mammals and some fish, this is usually a day length signal. Deer mate as the days become shorter in autumn, birds as the days become longer in spring. Sometimes the day length simply makes them ready to breed, but the temperature has to be warm enough before breeding is actually switched on.

Once an animal starts breeding, its internal clock takes over, and switches off breeding behaviour after a certain time. In rooks, which produce only one brood, the sex organs start to shrink after 6 weeks. Quails can go on mating and laying eggs for 4 months, and often produce several broods.

Journey to parenthood

Some animals travel to special breeding areas to produce their young. Birds, caribou and reindeer migrate north to breed. Fish like herring and cod migrate to special spawning grounds, where the water is warm and shallow and full of nutrients for the young fish. Like mating itself, these migrations are carefully timed by an internal clock. They are switched on by signals like day length and water temperature.

▼ Horseshoe crabs spawn at high tide on a North American beach.

Living in two worlds

Some animals have to migrate to breed. Adult frogs, toads, newts and salamanders live on land, feeding on insects and other small invertebrates. But when they mate, they must shed their sperm and eggs into the water. Their offspring, tadpoles, are little fish-like animals that breathe with gills and swim using their flexible tails. So frogs and their relatives must return to water to breed.

The sea turtles have the opposite problem. They need to lay their eggs on land. They bury them in a sandy beach, where the warmth of the sun will help them to hatch quickly.

More about Timing of reproduction p 22-23, 31, 47, 50-51 Young animals p 36, 50, 55
Breeding migrations p 34, 37, 47, 50, 54

Safety in numbers

Baby animals are an easy catch for many predators. If the animals in a population produce their young at exactly the same time, predators cannot eat them all at once, so more young survive.

Babies on the run

The young of animals like wildebeest and zebra, which live in large herds that are constantly on the move, are able to walk a few minutes after they are born. The wildebeest in the herd all give birth within about 3 days, so there are far more young than the local lions and hyaenas can take.

▲ A wildebeest with its newborn young. The baby is able to walk just a few hours after birth.

Gannets galore

Gannets, terns and many other seabirds nest in huge colonies on the cliff-tops. There is safety in numbers — more pairs of eyes on the look-out for danger. The alarm is soon given if an egg-thieving gull or skua appears on the scene. Many adult birds fly up to drive off the intruder. Day length signals cause the gannets to migrate to their breeding colonies at the same time, and the same signals synchronize their mating and egg-laying.

◀ Safety in numbers — in a gannet colony there are many pairs of eyes to look out for danger.

SAFETY IN NUMBERS

Sex in the sea

Many marine animals shed their sex cells into the water. The eggs and sperms must meet for a new individual to be produced. It is therefore an advantage for large numbers of sex cells to be produced at the same time and in the same place.

Animals like oysters, mussels and starfish, which are confined to the sea bed, produce special chemicals at certain times of the year. These stimulate all the animals in the area to release their millions of sperms and eggs into the water at the same time, until the sea turns cloudy.

Palolo worms live in the oceans. They use a moon clock. All the palolo worms in a particular area spawn (release their eggs) at the same time of year, always at dawn at the start of the last quarter of the moon. The sea becomes a vast wriggling green and brown mass of worms, a feast for sharks and other fish.

All together ... now

Many insect pupae all hatch at the same time. Along a particular stretch of river, mayflies and dragonflies all emerge at the same time. Local predators find more than enough to eat, so survival chances are better. The dragonflies all use a moon clock set to the same time.

Fruit flies always emerge at a particular time around dawn. Before their skins harden, they can dry out very easily, and the air is usually moist at dawn. They use an internal clock combined with the signal of light at sunrise.

When the sea turns pink

On Australia's Great Barrier Reef, many different kinds of corals all spawn at the same time, just 4 days after full moon in November. This mass of spawning occurs along nearly 900 km (558 miles) of reef. At this time, the tides are at their lowest, so there is little water movement over the reef, and the sperm and eggs are not washed away so quickly.

◀ Lit up by a diver's lamp, sponges release clouds of sperm into the water.

More about ▷ Safety in numbers p 17 Seabirds p 32, 36, 38
Spawning p 31, 47, 49

Changing colour

▲ Willow ptarmigans in winter (left) and in summer (right).

Some animals change colour at different times of year, so that the colour of their coats keeps pace with the changing colour of their surroundings. Birds and mammals shed their feathers or fur and grow new coats. Insects regularly shed their skins as they grow. The new skin may be a different colour from the old one. Many of these changes are triggered by external signals.

Stoat in winter white

Stoat in summer brown

Winter white

Animals like hares, stoats and ptarmigan, which live in the far north, change colour in autumn. When the day length decreases in late summer and autumn, they moult and grow a paler, thicker winter coat. This helps camouflage them against the snow.

Animals living in the far north turn white earlier than those living further south. Here, the snow arrives sooner. In Scotland and parts of northern Europe, temperature also helps to control coat colour in some animals. Scottish stoats turn white only in very severe winters.

CHANGING COLOUR

Light at night

Fiddler crabs have a daily rhythm of colour change which also varies with the state of the tides. At night, they remain pale, but by day they turn darker. At low tide in daylight, when they are at greatest risk from hungry birds, they become darker still. The darker colour helps to camouflage them against the dark mud. Their internal clock makes them change colour *before* they leave their burrows, so they gain extra protection.

▲ Fiddler crabs stay close to home while they scavenge for food on the mud.

Matchmaking

During summer, many plants gradually dry out and turn from green to brown. Some insects change colour to match. A signal from their background determines which colour they will have after each moult of skin. If moved from one background to another, they will change colour at their next moult.

Owl butterfly caterpillars are green in early summer, but when they moult in late summer, their new skins are brown. Grasshoppers are often green in early summer, and brown later on. Some grasshoppers from the African savanna can even produce black forms after the grass has been burnt. Swallowtail and cabbage white butterflies produce green pupae (chrysalids) in the early summer, but in late summer they produce brown pupae. These overwinter in safety hanging from bare twigs.

Wet and dry colours

Many animals change colour as the moisture in the air increases or decreases, or as the temperature rises. Toads become paler in dry, warm weather. Patches of dark pigment (coloured chemicals) in the toad's skin contract (shrink), so the skin looks paler. Pale colours reflect more heat than dark colours, helping to keep the toad cool. Such colour changes are common in desert lizards, too. Some praying mantids turn brown in dry air. In their natural habitat, the leaves on which they sit would soon turn brown in dry weather.

More about ▶ Winter coats p 25 Seasonal rhythms p 9, 13, 15, 21-23, 38, 48-50
Changing appearances p 9, 54-55

Changing shape and style

Some animals come in more than one shape and size, according to the time of year. Others change their lifestyle and habitat at a certain age. Many of these changes depend on signals from the animal's surroundings.

From river to sea ...

Salmon and eels migrate thousands of kilometres across the oceans at certain stages in their lives. Young salmon live in rivers, and usually face upstream, so that they are not swept out to sea. Once they reach a certain size, long days or warm water temperatures cause a change in habits. They swim downstream to the river mouth. Here, they develop a preference for salt water, and swim out to sea. After 3 or 4 years at sea, they return to their home river, perhaps 5000 km (3000 miles) away, to mate and lay their eggs.

How they find their way is still a mystery. Perhaps they follow ocean currents, or use a sun compass or a magnetic compass. Closer to home, their keen sense of smell detects the faint scent of their home river, or of their relatives living there.

▲ A salmon leaps a waterfall.

... and sea to river

The common eel has the opposite lifestyle. It lays its eggs in the Sargasso Sea, a giant eddy in the mid-Atlantic Ocean. The tiny leaf-like eel larvae drift north on the Gulf Stream for several years until they reach the coast and return to the rivers from which their parents came.

Here, they grow into 'yellow eels'. Eventually, they grow fat and become 'silver eels'. They can now live in salt water, and return to the ocean. During this change, their sense of direction alters, too. Yellow and silver eels will swim in opposite directions if placed in the ocean.

▼ Yellow and silver eels have different senses of direction.

yellow eel

silver eel

CHANGING SHAPE AND STYLE

To fly or not to fly?

Aphids, or greenfly, survive the winter as resting eggs. In spring, these hatch into winged aphids, which fly off to find suitable plants to feed on. In response to the long days of summer, when food is plentiful, the aphids multiply rapidly. They give birth to wingless aphids. This saves energy, as more new aphids can be produced from the same amount of food.

As the days shorten in late summer, the aphids produce winged offspring. These fly away to find suitable places to mate and lay their eggs. Overcrowding, and ageing of the leaves on which they feed, will also lead to winged offspring. These can then escape to find new plants.

▲ Aphids give birth to wingless offspring in spring.

Sink or swim

Many animals that live on the sea bed — starfish, sea urchins, crabs, lobsters, barnacles, mussels — produce tiny swimming larvae. They swim towards the light, to the surface of the sea, and live among the plankton. Here, they drift on the ocean currents until eventually they change into miniature adults. Now, they swim away from the light and settle out on the sea bed. This change in shape and lifestyle means that slow-moving crabs and starfish, and non-moving barnacles and mussels can colonize new areas of the sea bed.

More about Ocean migrations p 33, 34, 37, 45, 49 Larvae p 31, 36 Up-and-down swimmers p 19

We use signals, too

Humans live in the same world as other animals, so it is not surprising that they also use internal clocks and external signals. There are daily changes in body temperature and appetite, in waking and sleeping, and in many body processes. We are often unaware of our natural rhythms because we live in cities and towns where our lives are ruled by the clock, not by the sun.

Jet lag

The most obvious human rhythm is that of sleep. Most human rhythms run in cycles of about 25 to 26 hours, but are adjusted to 24 hours by the signals of dawn and dusk. This fine tuning is drastically upset when we fly around the world — hence the condition called jet lag.

When we cross time zones, our rhythms are still running at the local time of the place we have just left. It can take several days for the rhythms to adjust to the new time. Some rhythms adjust faster than others, so our body processes may become out of phase with each other. This is what makes us feel tired and unwell.

◀ It is no use being a milkman if you are not an early riser!

Rise and shine

We all know that some people just cannot get up in the morning, while others are irritatingly cheerful at dawn. This is because they have different sleep rhythms. By giving a late riser a 26.7-hour day, you can convert him or her into an early riser.

WE USE SIGNALS, TOO

Altering the clock

Humans alter the biological clocks of other animals and plants for their own advantage. By giving them long days, we can get chrysanthemums to flower at Christmas, and hens to keep laying eggs through the winter. For thousands of years, the Japanese have practised Yogai — giving songbirds long days to bring them into breeding condition so that they will sing.

Moonshine

Human births and deaths run in cycles. Women release their eggs once in every lunar month, yet there are peaks of births at particular times of year. Babies are most likely to be born soon after dawn, and deaths are more common in winter. People used to think that madness was related to the phases of the moon — hence the word 'lunatic'.

Human magnets

Humans have magnetic material just behind their noses. Blindfolded students taken many kilometres from home find their way back more accurately than students without a blindfold — they use their internal magnetic compass instead of visual cues. When wearing hats containing magnets, their sense of direction is even worse. Students who sleep with their feet pointing north or south have a better sense of direction than those who sleep in an east/west position. Presumably the Earth's magnetic field upsets their internal magnets.

Time to be ill

You are far more likely to have a heart attack or stroke at 9 am than at 9 pm. Your immune system also has a daily cycle. Hayfever is worst first thing in the morning, while asthma is worst at night. Asthma is worse in autumn than in spring, regardless of what sets it off. Alcohol and drugs are more effective at some times of day than at others. Responses to radiations, poisons and noise also vary through the day.

More about ▶▶ Daily rhythms p 10–15, 18, 19, 53 Biological clocks p 12, 13, 16, 57
Magnetic sense p 41, 44–45

57

Bibliography

The Rhythms of Life, Eds. Edward S. Ayensu and Philip Whitfield, Marshall Editions, 1982.

Survival in the Animal World, FRANZ GEISER and HANS DOSSENBACH, Orbis, 1985.

Nature Day and Night, RICHARD ADAMS, Kestrel Books/Penguin Books, 1978.

Unlocking Nature's Secrets, MICHAEL BRIGHT, BBC, 1984.

The Discovery of Animal Behaviour, JOHN SPARKS, Collins, 1982.

Bird Migration, CHRIS MEAD, Country Life Books, 1983.

Mimicry and Camouflage, JILL BAILEY, Hodder & Stoughton, 1988.

Biological Clocks, Their Functions in Nature, JOHN CLOUDSLEY-THOMPSON, Weidenfeld & Nicolson, 1980 (rather advanced).

Glossary

algae: simple plant-like growths with no obvious leaves or stems. Algae include seaweeds and millions of microscopic creatures that float near the surface of lakes and oceans.

axis: an imaginary straight line around which an object spins. The Earth's axis passes through both North and South poles.

cocoon: a fluffy ball of silk made by an animal.

diurnal: describes an animal that is active only during the daytime.

dormant: describes an organism that is resting and not growing.

emigration: the moving of animals in large numbers away from the main population, usually in response to overcrowding or food shortage.

germinate: to sprout and grow.

gills: structures used for breathing under water.

hibernation: a very deep sleep which helps an animal survive cold weather.

hormones: chemicals produced by living things. They are used to co-ordinate body processes.

invertebrates: animals without backbones.

larvae: young animals that look quite different from their parents. For example, tadpoles are the larvae of frogs.

light intensity: the brightness of light.

lunar: describes something relating to the moon.

mammals: warm-blooded (endothermic) animals with backbones, whose bodies are usually covered with fur or hair. Female mammals give birth to live young and feed them on milk.

migration: the movement of animals from one place to another, often over very long distances.

moulting: the process of shedding an outer covering of skin, shell, scales, fur or feathers.

mucus: a slimy fluid produced by animals. Mucus moistens and protects delicate surfaces and prevents them drying out.

neap tides: the lowest tides, caused when the sun and moon are at right angles, so that their gravitational pulls partly cancel each other out.

nectar: a sweet sugary liquid made by some flowers.

nocturnal: describes an animal that is active at night.

oxygen: a gas that is found in air and water. It has no colour, taste or smell. It is necessary for plant and animal life.

plankton: microscopic animals and plants that float near the surface of lakes and seas.

polarized light: light in which the light waves vibrate in only one plane.

pollen: tiny yellow, orange or red grains produced by the male parts of flowering and cone-bearing plants. The pollen grains contain the male sex cells.

predators: animals that hunt and eat other animals

prey: animals that are hunted and eaten as food by other animals

pupa: a stage in the life cycle of an insect in which the animal changes from a caterpillar to an adult insect. The pupa is often covered in a hard case. Inside, the body materials of the caterpillar are rearranged to form the adult butterfly, moth or fly.

roosting: describes birds that are resting or sleeping.

spawning: releasing eggs and sperm into water.

spawning ground: a special place where spawning takes place.

spring tides: the highest tides, formed when the sun and moon line up to exert the maximum pull of gravity.

stamens: the male parts of the flower, which produce the pollen grains.

sub-tropics: the regions just north and south of the tropics.

temperate regions: regions with mild winters and cool summers.

territory: a particular area of land or water in which an animal or group of animals live, feed and breed.

torpor: the condition of being very sleepy and inactive.

tubers: underground plant stems which are swollen with stored food.

tundra: a vast flat treeless part of the Arctic, where the soil is permanently frozen not far below the surface.

vertebrates: animals with backbones.

Index

adders 35
African hedgehogs 26
albatross 38
algae 45
ants 42
ants, leafcutter 42
  Pharaoh 42
aphids 29, 32, 39, 55
apple trees 6, 7
Arctic tern 32
armadillos 27

badgers 7, 8, 16, 24
barley 23
barnacles 55
Barrow ground
  squirrel 27
bat hawk 17
bats 8, 11, 26
bear, brown 27
  grizzly 25
  polar 25
bears 24, 25, 27
bees 40, 41, 45
beetles 35
biological clock 12, 13, 16, 57
bison 33
blackcaps 43
bluebells 24
bluetit 15
bonito 33
brown bear 27
bugs 29, 32
bullfrog 30
bushbabies 9
butterflies 24, 32, 38, 53
butterflies, cabbage
  white 53
  monarch 32, 38
  owl 53
  swallowtail 53

cabbage white
  butterflies 53
caribou 33, 34, 49

cats 11
cheetahs 8
chickadees 8
chipmunks 24, 27
chrysanthemums 57
coat-of-mail shells 45
cocklebur 22
cocoons 8, 24
cod 49
compass termites 44
compass,
  electromagnetic 38, 44, 45, 54, 57
  moon 42, 43
  star 43
  sun 39, 41, 43, 45, 54
coral reefs 18
corals 9, 51
crabs 8, 18, 47, 53, 55
  fiddler 53
  ghost 18
  horseshoe 47
  king 47
  shore 47
  spider 8, 18
crickets 29

daffodils 24
daily rhythms 10–15, 18, 19, 53, 56, 57
daisies 14, 15, 24
damselflies 51
dandelions 14, 15
dawn chorus 14, 15
deer 33, 48, 49
deserts 30, 31, 35, 48
diatoms 19
dogs 11
dolphins 45
dormouse 6, 24, 26
dragonflies 51
ducklings 48
ducks 34

earthworms 16, 18
eels 54

electromagnetic
  compass 38
elephants 48
elk 33
emigration 35
European hedgehog 17, 26
evening primrose 14
eyesight 8

feather stars 8, 18
fiddler crabs 53
finches 9
fish 8, 10, 11, 18, 19, 31, 33, 37, 42, 45, 47, 49, 51
flashlight fish 19
flycatchers 8, 9
four o'clock plant 15
foxes 12, 30
frogs 25, 27, 30, 31, 49
fruit flies 51
fur seal 33

gannets 44, 50
garden warblers 39
garter snake 30, 35
geese 34
gerbils 6, 27, 30
ghost crabs 18
giraffe 11, 17
goats 33
grasshoppers 53
gravity 43, 46
grey squirrel 10
grey whale 33
grizzly bear 25
ground squirrel 24, 27, 28
  Barrow 27
  mantled 27
grunion 47
gulls 50

hamster 6, 26
hares 8, 52

hawks 6, 17
hedgehogs 8, 16, 17, 26
  African 26
  European 17, 26
hens 57
herring 49
hibernation 21, 24, 26, 27
homing pigeons 39
honeybees 40, 41, 45
horseshoe crabs 47
hummingbirds 28

insects 6, 9, 14, 23–25, 28, 29, 31, 34, 36, 37, 39, 47, 51, 53
internal clock 7, 10, 19, 23, 28, 39, 40, 47, 49, 51, 53
irises 22

jet lag 56

kangaroo rats 30
king crabs 47

ladybirds 29
lanternfish 19
Laysan albatross 38
leafcutter ants 42
lemmings 35
lettuce 29
lichens 34
limpets 42
lions 17
lizards 53
lobsters 55
locusts 35, 48
lunar clock 46
lunar rhythms 46, 47, 51
lungfish 31
lupin 28

INDEX

magnetic compass 44, 45, 54, 57
magnetism 40, 41, 57
manatees 11
mantled ground squirrel 27
marmots 6, 27
marsupials 28
mice 24–28, 35, 48
midges 31, 47
migration 9, 21–23, 32–36, 38, 39, 42–45, 49, 54
molluscs 45
monarch butterflies 32, 38
moon 6, 13, 46, 47
moon clock 51
moon compass 42, 43
moose 33
mosquitoes 19
moths 8, 24, 29, 32
moulting 37, 52
mountain goat 21
mountain quail 33
mussels 51, 55

navigation 38–45, 57
nectar 14
newts 49
nocturnal animals 8, 9, 16, 17, 42

opossums 17, 27
owl 17
owl butterflies 53
oysters 51

palolo worms 51
parrotfish 10
Pharaoh ants 42
pigeons 39, 44, 45
  homing 39
plaice 36
plankton 19, 55
polarized light 40, 43

pollen 14
poppies 24
porpoises 45
potatoes 24
prawns 19
praying mantids 53
primroses 22
ptarmigans 52

quails 49
  mountain 33

rats 35
red squirrel 27
rooks 49

salamanders 27, 44, 45, 49
salmon 54
sandhoppers 6, 7, 18, 39, 42, 43, 47
scarlet pimpernel 15
scorpions 30
sea anemones 18
sea turtles 37, 49
sea urchins 55
sea-lions 11
sea-otters 11
seals 11
  fur 33
seashore midges 47
seasonal rhythms 9, 13, 15, 21–23, 38, 48–50
seeds 23, 24, 26, 28, 29, 31
sensitive plant 12
sharks 37, 51
sheep 33
shore crabs 47
shrews 16, 48
shrimps 31, 36, 47
skua 50
sleep 8, 10–13, 17, 24, 26, 28, 31, 56
sloths 27
slugs 11, 16

snails 11, 16, 31
snakes 27, 35
  garter 30, 35
spider crabs 8, 18
spring peeper 25
squid 18, 19
squirrels 10, 26, 27
  grey 10
  red 27
star compass 43
starfish 51, 55
stoats 52
sun compass 39, 41, 43, 45, 54
swallows 6, 7, 9, 23, 34, 36
swallowtail butterflies 53
swifts 11, 23, 36

tadpoles 31, 49
tanagers 9
termites 44, 45
terns 50
  Arctic 32
thrushes 9
tide 6, 7, 13, 18, 46, 47
tits 8, 15
toads 31, 47, 49, 53
tobacco 14
torpor 28
tuna 37
turtles 27, 28, 37, 49

voles 12, 24

waders 34
waggle dance 41
warblers 8, 9, 23, 34, 39, 43
  garden 39
weasels 52
weaver birds 21
whales 11, 33, 34, 45
  grey 33
wheat 23, 29

whippoorwill 28
wildebeest 34, 50
wolf 25
woodlice 30

yaks 25
Yogai 57

Acknowledgements

ARTISTS:

Patrick and Tammy Duffin/Linden Artists; Adam Hook/Linden Artists; Steve Lings/Linden Artists; Mick Loates/Linden Artists; Alan Male/Linden Artists; Jane Pickering/Linden Artists; Maurice Pledger/Linden Artists; Sebastian Quigley/Linden Artists; Sallie Alane Reason; John Rignall/Linden Artists; Clive Spong/Linden Artists; Helen Townson; David Webb/Linden Artists and BLA Publishing

PHOTOGRAPHIC CREDITS:

t = top; b = bottom; c = centre; l = left; r = right.

COVER: Andy Purcell/Bruce Coleman Ltd. 6t & b John Shaw/NHPA. 7 Alfred Albinger/Frank Lane Picture Agency. 8 Mark N. Boulton/Bruce Coleman Ltd. 9 Anthony Bannister/NHPA. 10t G.I. Bernard/Oxford Scientific Films. 10b Alan Power/Bruce Coleman Ltd. 11 Trevor Hill. 12 Stephen Dalton/NHPA. 14 W.T. Davidson/Frank Lane Picture Agency. 15 Roger Wilmshurst/Frank Lane Picture Agency. 16t Hans Reinhard/Bruce Coleman Ltd. 16b Trevor Hill. 17 Alastair Shay/Oxford Scientific Films. 18 Leo Collier/Seaphot. 19 Jimmy Wilmot/Seaphot. 20 Oxford Scientific Films. 21 Jeff Foott/Survival Anglia. 22 John Shaw/Bruce Coleman Ltd. 23 D. Kinzler/Frank Lane Picture Agency. 24 Geoff Dove/Bruce Coleman Ltd. 25t Hans Reinhard/Bruce Coleman Ltd. 25b Keith Gunnar/Bruce Coleman Ltd. 26 Rocco Longo/Bruce Coleman Ltd. 27t G.D.T./NHPA. 27b Harry Teyn/NHPA. 28 John Shaw/Bruce Coleman Ltd. 29 Keith Gunnar/Bruce Coleman Ltd. 30 Bob and Clara Calhoun/Bruce Coleman Ltd. 31 Anthony Bannister/NHPA. 32t Geoff Dove/Bruce Coleman Ltd. 32b Ron Austing/Frank Lane Picture Agency. 33 Steven C. Kaufman/Bruce Coleman Ltd. 34t Steve McCutcheon/Frank Lane Picture Agency. 34b Agence Nature/NHPA. 35 Anthony Bannister/NHPA. 36t Stephen Dalton/NHPA. 36b Jany Sauvanet/NHPA. 38t Frans Lanting/Bruce Coleman Ltd. 38b Stephen Dalton/NHPA. 40 Kim Taylor/Bruce Coleman Ltd. 41 David Thompson/Oxford Scientific Films. 42t Peter Crassweller. 42b Stephen Dalton/NHPA. 43 David George/Seaphot. 44t Ken Lucas/Seaphot. 44b, 45 A.N.T./NHPA. 46 Steve McCutcheon/Frank Lane Picture Agency. 47 Jeff Foot/Bruce Coleman Ltd. 48t Hans Reinhard/Bruce Coleman Ltd. 48b E.A. MacAndrew/NHPA. 49 Leonard Lee Rue III/Bruce Coleman Ltd. 50t Jonathan Scott/Seaphot. 50b R. Tidman/Frank Lane Picture Agency. 51t John Shaw/Bruce Coleman Ltd. 51b Peter Scoones/Seaphot. 52l Mark Newman/Frank Lane Picture Agency. 52r John Shaw/NHPA. 53 C.B. Frith/Bruce Coleman Ltd. 54 Brian Hawkes/NHPA. 55 Kim Taylor/Bruce Coleman Ltd. 56 Clive D. Woodley/Bruce Coleman Ltd.